CLIMATE Change
PROBLEMS and PROGRESS

The Future of Biodiversity

CLIMATE Change
PROBLEMS and PROGRESS

CLIMATE Change

PROBLEMS and PROGRESS

The Future of Biodiversity

James Shoals

Mason Crest

Mason Crest
450 Parkway Drive, Suite D
Broomall, PA 19008
www.masoncrest.com

Series ISBN: 978-1-4222-4353-4
Hardback ISBN: 978-1-4222-4356-5
EBook ISBN: 978-1-4222-7451-4

First printing
1 3 5 7 9 8 6 4 2

Cover photographs by Dreamstime.com: Kostya Pazyuk (bkgd); Chase Dekker (top left); Richard Carey (bottom); Maiphone Yang (right).

Names: Shoals, James, author.
Title: The future of biodiversity / by James Shoals.
Description: Broomall, PA : Mason Crest, [2019] | Series: Climate challenges: problems and progress | Includes bibliographical references and index.
Identifiers: LCCN 2019013881| ISBN 9781422243565 (hardback) | ISBN 9781422243534 (series) | ISBN 9781422274514 (ebook)
Subjects: LCSH: Biodiversity--Juvenile literature. | Nature--Effect of human beings on--Juvenile literature. | Climatic changes--Juvenile literature. | Endangered species--Juvenile literature.
Classification: LCC QH541.15.B56 S56 2019 | DDC 333.95--dc23 LC record available at https://lccn.loc.gov/2019013881

CONTENTS

KEY ICONS TO LOOK FOR

Words to Understand: These words with their easy-to-understand definitions will increase the reader's understanding of the text, while building vocabulary skills.

Sidebars: This boxed material within the main text allows readers to build knowledge, gain insights, explore possibilities, and broaden their perspectives by weaving together additional information to provide realistic and holistic perspectives.

Educational Videos: Readers can view videos by scanning our QR codes, providing them with additional educational content to supplement the text. Examples include news coverage, moments in history, speeches, iconic moments, and much more!

Text-Dependent Questions: These questions send the reader back to the text for more careful attention to the evidence presented here.

Research Projects: Readers are pointed toward areas of further inquiry connected to each chapter. Suggestions are provided for projects that encourage deeper research and analysis.

Series Glossary of Key Terms: This back-of-the-book glossary contains terminology used throughout this series. Words found here increase the reader's ability to read and comprehend higher-level books and articles in this field.

atmosphere the blanket of gases enveloping the Earth

calcium carbonate a white, solid compound found in chalk, limestone, and in animal shells and bones

climate the weather conditions of a particular place

dengue fever a disease caused by viruses spread by mosquitoes, involving high fever, rashes on the body, headache, and vomiting

disrupt to interrupt or stop something

endangered an organism that is facing danger and is about to go extinct

environment the surroundings or conditions in which a person, animal, or plants live

extinction the process of an animal or plant no longer existing

habitat the natural home or environment of a living organism.

immune system the body's defense system that fights germs to prevent infections and diseases

incubation a process to keep eggs warm till the time babies develop and come out

krill a very small shrimp-like crustacean

lichen a very small, soft, and slow-growing plant

malaria a mosquito-borne disease producing fevers, chills, and flu-like symptoms in humans

malnutrition a medical condition in which an animal or person does not get enough nutrients in his/her diet

metabolism a process by which food is converted into energy

mortality rate the measurement of number of deaths against the population of an area

moss soft green or brown plant that grows in layers on wet ground, rocks, or trees

passerine related to birds known for having feet most suitable for perching on trees

permafrost ground that remains permanently frozen all year round

plankton very tiny organisms that include both zooplankton and phytoplankton

precipitation water that falls to the ground in the form of either rain, snow, hail, or sleet

spawn the release or deposition of eggs by a fish, frog, mollusk, etc.

symbiotic relationship a relationship between two living organisms in which each benefits the other

thaw when ice or snow turns liquid due to high temperature

tundra the Arctic region of Asia, Europe, and North America

vulnerable someone or something that can be easily harmed or attacked

waterfowl birds that spend most of their life in or near water

INTRODUCTION

Biodiversity is the sum total of all living organisms inhabiting the Earth. It refers to the variety and variation in living organisms, their species and their habitats. Global warming and climate change have emerged as great threats to biodiversity.

As the planet is warming up, plants and animals are trying to adapt to their changing environments. However, the pace of change is so fast that some living organisms are not able to cope with the challenges. This is making some species vulnerable to **extinction**. Not only rising temperatures but also changes in rainfall patterns, breeding seasons, as well as the reducing interaction between animals and plants have endangered many species. It is believed that if global temperatures rise by over 3.5°F (2°C), up to 70 percent of the world's known species would go extinct.

It's Warming Up!

The Earth is heating up due to global warming. Rising temperatures, changes in precipitation patterns, melting polar ice, rising sea levels, and drying rivers and lakes are some of the adverse effects of global warming. It is also pushing certain species on planet Earth to the brink of extinction.

The Arctic and Antarctica

The Arctic and Antarctica remain covered with ice for most of the year. However, due to soaring temperatures, these ice reserves are melting. In Antarctica, a chunk of ice larger than the state of New York was headed for collapse in 2019. Many scientists think that the ice shelf was weakened by the warm winds blowing over it.

Rivers

The Ganges in India, which is fed by the Gangotri Glacier, is beginning to run dry because the glacier is shrinking. It is shrinking at a rate of 40 yards (36 m) per year, almost twice as fast as twenty years ago. Many scientists say that the glacier will disappear by 2030.

Lakes

Due to global warming, many lakes of the world have dried up, or are in the process of drying up. Lake Cachet in Chile disappeared completely, leaving a large puddle in 2008. The water levels of Lake Superior, the world's largest freshwater reservoir, have also fallen drastically.

Climate Facts

- The number of glaciers in Glacier National Park has dropped from 150 to twenty-six since 1850. It is estimated that within the next twenty-five to thirty years, all the remaining glaciers will melt.

- There are about a hundred million species on Earth, out of which only 1.4 million have been identified.

Changing Oceans and Seas

Global warming is affecting the composition of oceans and seas as well as the living organisms that thrive in them. Plankton (zooplankton and phytoplankton), seagrass, and kelp forests are greatly affected by the rise in water temperatures and carbon dioxide levels.

Kelp Forests

Kelps are large seaweed. Kelp forests are areas that have a high density of this seaweed. These areas are some of the most popular habitats among marine organisms. They provide shelter as well as food to a wide variety of fish, lobsters, sea otters, seals, sea urchins, sea stars, jellyfish, and many others. Kelp needs cold water to grow, but with rising sea temperatures, their survival is becoming a struggle.

Phytoplankton

Phytoplankton are a major food source for many organisms. They are small, plantlike organisms that drift in water. Like land plants, phytoplankton make their own food through the process of photosynthesis. They grow faster in colder waters and slower in warmer ocean waters. If the growth of phytoplankton becomes slow due to the warming of the oceans, then there would be less food for animals such as fish, marine birds, and mammals.

Seagrass

Seagrass is the only flowering plant that lives completely submerged in coastal waters. Seagrass meadows are popular nursery grounds for many fish species, crustaceans, and other organisms. Rising sea and carbon dioxide levels are making seagrasses vulnerable to extinction. If seagrasses continue to face such risks due to global warming, then organisms that depend on them for food such as sea turtles, manatees, dugongs, seabirds, sea urchins, and others, will also come under threat.

Climate Facts

- Areas in the oceans and seas with very low oxygen to support life are called "dead zones." The rise in temperatures has increased the number of dead zones.

- Phytoplankton produce half of the oxygen that the world breathes.

Struggling Life in the Oceans

The distribution, abundance, and variety of marine life are changing due to global warming. Temperatures and the absorption of carbon dioxide by the oceans and seas are on the rise. Higher carbon dioxide content is making marine waters acidic. This is affecting marine species and is a grave threat to their survival.

Coral Reefs

Coral reefs are home to more than 25 percent of all marine life. They are formed by tiny organisms called coral polyps. Rising sea temperatures have proved to be fatal for coral reefs as they affect the growth of the algae that depend on a **symbiotic relationship** with the reefs and provide them with food. Warm temperatures and less oxygen make the corals expel the algae, which causes them to turn white and die. This is called coral bleaching.

Fish

With the rise in temperature and oxygen deficiency, the life cycles of fish are affected in a disturbing way. Some fish are reproducing early, while in others, the process has delayed. The time span of egg hatching has also changed along with the growth rate and shifts in **spawning** season. Additionally, some species of fish, such as Pacific salmon, are so vulnerable to climate change that it is affecting their **metabolism**. The warmer the water, the more food they need to eat.

Sea Turtles

Warmer temperatures could lessen the number of male sea turtle offspring and threaten the sea turtle population. The sex of the sea turtle hatchlings depends on the temperature of water. Warmer temperatures could lead to a decline in the birth of sea turtles.

Climate Facts

- According to reports, ocean acidification is making clownfish hard of hearing.

- Scientific studies have predicted that the Great Barrier Reef could lose up to 95 percent of its corals by 2050 because of global warming.

S ince the beginning of the Industrial Revolution, acidity in the seas has increased by 30 percent. Several effects of this acidification have already caused irreversible damage to marine life. In fact, climate scientists claim that these effects are likely to accelerate. If carbon dioxide (CO_2) emissions continue to harm key parts of the marine environment at the present rate, some sea species may face extinction by 2050.

Marine Calcifiers

There are certain marine animals such as mollusks, corals, crustaceans, and others that create their shells with the help of **calcium carbonate**. Such organisms are called marine calcifiers. However, the increasing carbon dioxide in water hampers the ability of these organisms to produce new shells. As oceans and seas are becoming acidic, shells of most marine calcifiers may also dissolve.

ABOUT 30 PERCENT OF THIS ODORLESS, INVISIBLE GAS IS ABSORBED BY THE OCEAN.

Ocean acidification explained

Whales

As the population of **plankton** declines, so animals feeding on plankton are threatened. The **mortality rate** of whales is very high due to less food available. It is also one of the reasons why whales are not giving birth to as many babies, as they need a proper diet and nutrition to carry young ones as well as for nursing. According to reports, killer whales have now been seen feeding on sea otters, which has never been a source of their food before. This shows that change in temperatures is also changing the habits of living organisms.

Lobsters

Lobsters are cold-blooded animals and their body temperature is determined by the temperature of the water they live in. A rise in temperature causes cold-blooded animals to use more energy for life processes such as respiration, growth, and reproduction. In the Gulf of Maine, the population of lobsters is on the rise as warmer water spurs a longer growing season, which encourages the speedy growth of these organisms. It causes lobsters to hatch earlier and provides better conditions for their larvae. On the other hand, the population of fish that feed on lobsters, such as cod, has declined due to global warming.

Climate Facts

- According to the IWC, only three hundred North Atlantic right whales are alive today.

- The world oceans are home to about three hundred to five hundred million living species.

Melting Poles

Polar bears, seals, walruses, and penguins are among the most populous animals of the poles. However, the melting sea ice has created problems for these polar animals. These animals are adapted to the extreme cold conditions and feed on other polar animals, such as the Antarctic cod, dragonfish, and ice fish.

Polar Bears

Polar bears are the largest carnivorous animals on land. They are up to 10 feet (3.2 tall and weigh up to 1,700 pounds (771 kg). Polar bears mostly feed on seals, cracking sea ice where seals may surface to breathe. With the polar ice melting away, polar bears are losing their hunting grounds. In addition, shorter periods of sea ice coverage give them less time to hunt.

Penguins

Penguins are flightless seabirds found in the Antarctic. They depend on sea ice and extreme cold temperatures to breed and grow. Emperor penguins do not make nests. They raise their chicks on the frozen sea, which usually takes about seven months. If the sea ice disappears before the chicks can learn to live on their own, then they will be swept into the sea. In addition, sea ice has been forming late and receding early, and is shrinking each winter. This has caused great harm to the penguins' **habitats**.

Seals

Seals make lairs in snow to keep their pups safe from predators. Rising temperatures are making the lairs melt before the pups are capable of surviving on their own. As the Southern Ocean and the Arctic are warming up, sea ice is melting and populations of fish and **krill** on which seals feed are declining.

Climate Facts

- According to research, polar bears have become skinnier due to scarcity of food.

- Population of Adélie penguins have gone down from thirty-two thousand breeding pairs to eleven thousand in the past thirty years.

Polar Life

A large variety of seabirds and plants, as well as Inuit people, call the polar regions home. Even a slight change in atmospheric temperature affects all the living organisms living there. While some living organisms are able to adapt to the changing temperatures, others are not able to do so.

Polar Plants

Mosses and **lichens** grow in polar regions. These plants are highly adaptable to the freezing cold **environment**. Other than that, Antarctic hair grass and Antarctic pearlwort are two native flowering plants that thrive in Antarctica. As temperatures rise, flowering plants are growing in areas that were earlier covered by ice sheets.

The Inuit

The Inuit are native to the Arctic. They largely depend on polar bear meat for food, and their skin to make clothes. However, as the population of polar bears is declining, the Inuit are running out of food and animal skin. Warmer weather has also reduced the number of hunting days. They are exposed to dangerous situations, such as thinning sea ice and **thawing permafrost**. They also find it hard to build igloos with less snow and ice.

Seabirds

Seabirds such as Arctic terns, Arctic skuas, and kittiwakes, among others, are facing food shortage as their primary food source, the sand eel, is declining. Consequently, nearly seven thousand pairs of great skuas in the Shetlands are producing only a handful of chicks. Moreover, starving adult birds have begun preying on their own young ones.

Climate Facts

- Mosses and lichens survive during extreme winters by dehydrating and producing antifreeze chemicals.

- Blowing cold winds have also shifted those ice formations that the Inuit have long used as landmarks for navigation.

Plants in Danger

As temperatures are rising, the risk of drastic changes in **precipitation**, forest fires, drought, and floods is also increasing. In some places, it is raining more than usual, while in others the rains are delayed. The timing of bud burst, leaf drop from trees, pollination, growth, and reproduction has also experienced changes.

Plants Cool the Earth

Plants and trees absorb carbon dioxide and give out oxygen for all living organisms to breathe. They also release water into the atmosphere through tiny pores present on their leaves. This makes the surrounding temperature cool. However, when the level of carbon dioxide increases in the atmosphere, these pores shrink and release less water, thus making the surrounding temperature warm.

Heat Waves and Frost Days

Heat waves as well as frost days last longer than usual due to global warming. This harms an array of plant species. Persistent warm summer is responsible for the increase in population of many insects, such as the spruce bark beetle, which has infested four million spruce trees in Alaska.

Droughts

Droughts are beginning to strike areas that normally have not been hit by droughts before. This causes many plants to receive less water and nutrients than they need to survive. Quiver trees, which are found in the Namib Desert in southern Africa, are dying and disappearing from their range due to droughts.

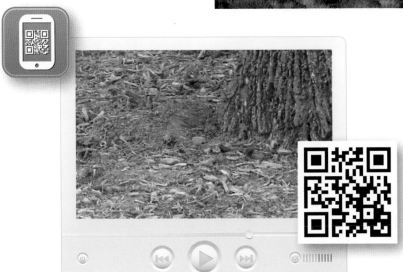

Impact of drought on trees

Climate Facts

- Poison ivy is a plant that causes itchy rashes to most people upon touching. With increasing levels of CO_2 in the atmosphere, scientists expect it to grow faster and become more toxic.

- Warmer temperatures in winter are causing some flowering plants to bloom early.

Forests at Risk

orests cover one-third of the Earth's surface and are home to hundreds of thousands of living organisms. Even small changes in temperature and precipitation levels have severe effects on forests as well as animals living there. They also increase the risk of forest fires, which burn large patches of land. There has been a drastic increase in wildfires over the years.

Trees on the Move

Increasing temperatures are compelling many living organisms to shift to areas with lower temperatures. As a result, plants and trees are also shifting towards the poles. American basswood, northern white cedar, black ash, sugar maple, yellow birch, and bigtooth aspen are headed north. Among all the trees mentioned, basswood and maple appear to have moved the most, by almost as much as 30 miles (50 km).

Changing Tree Lines

Climatic conditions determine the tree line—the natural borderline to which trees are capable of growing—and tree lines can in turn affect the **climate** of a region. Usually, trees grow as far north as they can until the climate becomes inhospitable for them to grow any further. Due to rising temperatures, tree lines are moving further up north where the overall natural climate is becoming stable and predictable for them to grow. They are also bringing along a greater diversity of wildlife and thus creating an imbalance in the native ecosystem.

Conserve Forests

Forests stock up to 80 percent of the carbon stored on land. If people keep cutting down trees for various purposes, then about 1.7 billion tons of carbon will be released into the atmosphere per year. Rainforests are one of the largest reservoirs of carbon dioxide and can help in reducing global warming. However, with the rise in carbon dioxide in the atmosphere, plants and trees in the Amazon rainforest are experiencing slow growth, and many are dying rapidly.

Climate Facts

- In a drought in 2005, the Amazon Basin released a billion tons of carbon dioxide into the atmosphere.

- Almost half of the Alpine plants on Mount Kosciuszko in Australia are threatened because of global warming.

Threat to Wildlife

Global warming is the greatest threat to the Earth's wildlife. The climate is changing so rapidly that many wildlife species are not being able to adapt quickly enough in order to breed or to migrate to more hospitable areas of the planet. Their food resources are also affected by the changing climatic patterns. Some studies have predicted that 37 percent of all plant and animal species may become extinct by 2050 due to climate change.

Lemurs

Changes in temperature and rainfall patterns can affect the ability of female lemurs to reproduce. They are not known to be active during heavy rains; hence, there are fewer chances of giving birth to babies. Also, heavy rains cause fruits to fall off, affecting food availability for baby lemurs. It becomes difficult for the infants to survive if they are not well fed. The Milne-Edwards' sifaka lemur found in Madagascar is threatened due to global warming.

Koala

Koalas only feed on the leaves of eucalyptus trees. Due to rise in carbon dioxide levels in the atmosphere, the nutrient balance in the trees is changing, making eucalyptus leaves unhealthy for koalas. Hence, koalas are eating food that does not give them enough energy to survive. As a result, the animals are facing extinction due to **malnutrition** or starvation.

Primates

The plants that grow in warmer temperatures have more fiber in their leaves and less digestible protein. Therefore, the animals that feed on leaves will take longer to digest their food. Higher temperatures also compel some gorillas and monkeys to stay in shade during the day instead of foraging for food, bonding with their group members, and protecting territories. This inactivity along with less nutritious food would ultimately drive mountain gorillas and colobus monkeys toward extinction.

Possums

The green ringtail possum is endemic to Queensland's tropical rainforests. This animal cannot regulate its body temperature when the ambient temperature rises above 104°F (40°C). Rising temperatures and heat waves could wipe out the possum population.

Climate Facts

• Global warming is making animals grow smaller. The Soay sheep found in Scotland is shrinking!

• Arctic foxes, elephants, tigers, orangutans, and several other animals are losing their habitats due to global warming.

Amphibians Facing Peril

Amphibians are animals that spend part of their lives in water and part on land. They are affected by even the slightest change in temperature. Amphibians are divided into groups: frogs and toads, salamanders, and newts.

Unsafe Amphibians

Amphibians have soft, moist skin covered by a layer of mucus. They stay near water to keep their bodies moist. Their skin is very thin which makes them **vulnerable** to minor changes in temperature, humidity, and air and water quality.

Effects on Amphibians

Rise in temperatures helps some bacteria and fungus to thrive, resulting in the outbreak of diseases. According to research, the **immune system** of amphibians is becoming increasingly weaker. Several bacteria are causing life-threatening diseases and the population of amphibians is declining. Usually, these animals feed on insects so if there are fewer amphibians then the insect population would increase. This could be dangerous.

Breeding

The breeding period of amphibians largely depends on the temperature and moisture in the environment. They lay jellylike, unshelled eggs that cannot survive dryness. Amphibians living in temperate regions around the world are facing the greatest threat due to global warming. Most of the animals living in these regions hibernate to escape hot summers or chilling winters. An increase in temperatures force them to come out of their hibernation and breed early. As frogs depend on water to breed, any change in rainfall can affect their reproduction. If they breed early in the season, they might become more vulnerable to snowmelt-induced floods and early winter.

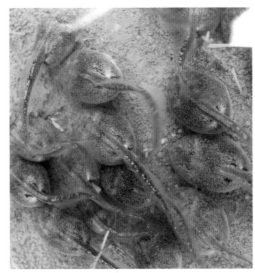

Climate Facts

• About two-thirds of the 110 harlequin frog species have gone extinct during the 1980s and 1990s.

• The Golden toad has gone extinct because of the increasing temperatures.

Reptiles in Trouble

Reptiles are cold-blooded and have scaly skin. Lizards, crocodiles, alligators, snakes, turtles, tortoises, and the like, are reptiles. As the climate is changing, reptiles are being forced to change their habitats and behaviors to survive global warming.

Effects on Reptiles

Like amphibians, reptiles respond quickly to changes in air and water quality and temperature, and the amount of rainfall. However, they are more mobile and have greater ability to bear drier and warmer temperatures than amphibians. Reptiles usually bask in the sun to stay warm and when the temperature becomes too hot, they seek shade to cool off. As temperatures are rising, reptiles stay in the shade for a longer time and spend less time looking for food.

Male or Female

Whether eggs will hatch into male or female baby reptiles depends entirely on the temperature at the time of **incubation**. Warmer temperatures result in the hatching of male reptiles whereas colder temperatures favor the hatching of female reptiles.

Breeding

The timing of breeding, and laying and hatching eggs may change because of the rise in temperature and the changes in rainfall patterns. Lizards reproduce during spring but they are not able to reproduce in high temperatures. Marine reptiles such as sea turtles are also affected as a rise in sea levels is posing a threat to their nesting grounds. Rises in air and water temperatures have also affected the reproduction of sea turtles.

Climate Facts

- The Galapagos tortoise, spiny lizard, desert tortoise, and others, are a few of the **endangered** reptile species.

- According to research, 20 percent of lizard species will go extinct by 2080.

Insects Around the World

nsects are one of the most biologically diverse species on Earth. They are very particular about their habitat and react quickly to any change in temperature. This is why insects are also known as environmental indicators.

Insects Facing Climate Hazards

Changes in temperature influence the behavior, distribution, life cycle, and reproduction of insects. As insects have shorter lifespans and high reproductive rates, they respond faster to climate change than do organisms that live longer, such as plants and animals. High temperatures are ideal for many insects to reproduce, leading to a rise in the population of insects, such as mosquitoes and beetles. These insects will affect humans and other living organisms adversely.

More than 40% of insect species are declining and one-third are endangered, according to the first global scientific review.

Insects and climate change

Insects and Pollination

Pollination is a process in which pollens from one flower are transferred to another flower. Insects such as bumblebees, butterflies, flies, and others, are a few of the main agents of pollination. The early season climate in many places is becoming warmer and drier, changing the flowering time in the area. Flowers are blooming early, at a time when insects are not there to pollinate. As a result, plants are not be able to reproduce, and by the time insects arrive, they do not get enough flowers to feed on.

Tropics and Temperate

In the tropics, the temperature remains constant throughout the year. This is why insects cannot adapt to changing temperatures, which might cause several species to go extinct. In temperate regions, insects are adapting to the changing temperature, increasing their population.

Climate Facts

- By 2050, more than a million living organisms, including some plants, will become extinct due to global warming.

- Seasons are extending due to global warming. According to a report, spring in Greenland is arriving much earlier than it did ten years ago.

Impact on Butterflies

Butterflies are one of the most beautiful insects. Like every other insect, butterflies also respond quickly to temperature changes. As the Earth heats up and the climate patterns change, butterflies are moving to places with a more favorable climate.

Effects on Butterflies

Butterflies are also reeling under the effects of climate change. In areas near sea level, their diversity is falling fast. The lowland species of butterflies are not only suffering due to warmer temperatures but are also facing habitat loss due to human activities. They are, therefore, moving up to higher and cooler altitudes. At the same time, the diversity of high-elevation butterflies that reside in colder regions is falling because they are finding it difficult to adapt to the warmer temperatures.

Benefitting Butterflies

Not all butterflies are at risk, as some butterfly species are taking advantage of changing climate. The brown argus butterfly has responded to climate change by changing its diet. Their population has flourished in Britain in the past twenty years, and the butterfly has become a common sight. The comma butterfly is growing in great numbers and expanding its range northwards. Similarly, the swallowtail butterfly is likely to expand its range further north, including northwestern Europe.

Monarch Migrations

Monarch butterflies of Canada and the United States migrate to Mexico and form colonies in mountains. There, they go into hibernation to avoid winter. After a few months, when the temperature rises and there is less humidity, the monarchs come down and return to the plains in the spring. Global warming is threatening their population by changing the climate. Wetter and colder winters as well as drier and hotter summers are harming the monarchs.

Climate Facts

- The populations of moths, crickets, and dragonflies have increased due to global warming in Britain.

- The monarch butterfly is also known as the milkweed butterfly and the wanderer butterfly.

Impact on Birds

T he rising temperatures are posing a threat to the habitat and food resources of birds. The change in the timings of different seasons are making birds respond to the early spring weather. This may lead them to fly north while there is still snow, and to where there is no availability of food.

What Will Happen?

Birds are adapted to a particular type of climate, vegetation, and habitat. With a rise in temperature, many birds are shifting to colder regions. Many birds such as the North American warbler and golden-winged warbler are moving northwards. Those birds that are not able to change habitat are at higher risk of becoming extinct. For example, the red-cockaded woodpecker in the southeastern United States lives in mature pine forests and not anywhere else. As the habitat cannot spread to new areas quickly or at all, the bird is endangered.

Changing Behavior

Rising temperatures are responsible for the changing behaviors of birds. The robins that reside in the Rocky Mountains are laying eggs approximately two weeks earlier in spring than they did several years ago. Worms and other food items on which robins feed are not yet available for their newly hatched babies. Many bird species in Britain have begun laying eggs earlier than usual as well.

Tropical Birds

Birds in the tropics are more vulnerable to changing climate. Droughts and irregular dry seasons are reducing their populations, which often breed in the wet season when food is available in great quantities. Toucans, found in Costa Rican lowlands, are shifting to cloud forests located at higher altitudes, competing with native birds, such as quetzals, for nest space in trees. Toucans are also feeding on eggs and nestlings of the native birds.

Climate Facts

• Wading birds, such as the ringed plover, used to spend winters on the west coast of Britain, but are now wintering in the east.

• According to studies, more that 80 percent of birds spend at least some time in the tropics.

Rising temperatures are causing unwanted changes in the timing of the natural cycles of animals and birds. The migration timings, places of migration, and even reproductive routines of birds are undergoing changes to adjust with the changing climate. Higher spring temperatures are drying up the breeding habitat of birds such as **waterfowl**.

Birds Are Shrinking

It may sound unbelievable but it is true. According to a study conducted by the Australian National University, the birds in southeastern Australia have become 2–4 percent smaller than their normal size. The size of these birds was compared with museum specimens of Australian birds. This change in their size has been linked to climate change because over the same century, the average daily temperatures in Australia rose steadily. The study concluded that birds are downsizing because smaller bodies shed heat faster than large ones.

Waterfowl

Waterfowl are greatly affected by global warming. Their habitats, food sources, and migration cycles are changing. The Prairie Pothole Region in the Great Plains is one of the most important breeding areas in North America. The region is now drying up due to longer dry seasons and drought, which is affecting the breeding of birds. The population of ducks, mallards, blue-winged teal, gadwall, canvasbacks, ruddy ducks, and northern pintails are declining.

Facing Potential Extinction

Some birds are changing their habitats to cope with the changing climate. However, those that cannot change their nesting places are vulnerable to extinction. **Passerine** birds such as the variegated fairy-wren, with a striking blue crown, and the yellow-rumped thornbill are threatened. Populations of the tawny eagle in Africa and Asia are declining because of changes in rainfall patterns.

Effect of climate change on birds

Climate Facts

- Rising temperatures are responsible for the low growth of puffin fledglings around the world.

- Migratory birds in the United Kingdom, such as chiffchaffs, have stopped migrating to the south and stay in the country throughout the year.

Impact on Migration

Animals across the globe migrate from one place to another to avoid harsh weather conditions, to find food, or to breed. They fly, walk, swim, or drift to reach their desired place. However, changes in temperature, precipitation levels, and season length are **disrupting** migration patterns and timings.

Threat to Migrating Animals

Migrating animals take cues from the environment to know when they should begin their journey. Rising temperatures, early springs, long and dry summers, and short and harsh winters are posing problems for many migrating animals. If they wait too long, these animals would not be able to stock up enough food before their departure. In addition, if the animals arrive at their destination early, they have to compete with animals already living there.

Storm Petrel

Storm petrels migrate from their breeding grounds in the North Atlantic to Namibia, South Africa, and the Indian Ocean. These birds must stock up large fat reserves to fuel their long voyage. Their ability to maintain and carry fat reserves depends on the climatic conditions as well as their migration route, which is adversely affected by global warming.

Siberian Crane

The Siberian crane is a migratory bird. These cranes are found in the Arctic **tundra** of western and eastern Russia. They are on the verge of extinction and only three thousand of them remain now. Due to global warming, the habitat of Siberian cranes is diminishing. The eastern population of cranes migrates to China during winters, whereas the western population migrates to Iran. Less precipitation along with heavy rainfall is also threatening the cranes in China.

Climate Facts

• The Siberian cranes used to spend winters in the Keoladeo National Park in India, but due to droughts and rising temperatures, they do not come to India anymore.

• Bar-tailed godwits make a nonstop flight, covering a distance of 6,800 miles (11,000 km) in eight days.

Impact on Hibernation

Hibernation is a state of deep sleep that an animal enters to avoid harsh, cold temperatures. Ground squirrels, bears, and chipmunks are hibernating animals. Temperature often tells animals when to go into hibernation and when to wake up. However, global warming is upsetting animal hibernation.

Threat

Most animals go into hibernation to avoid extreme cold, which makes it difficult for them to find food. During hibernation, these animals survive on stored energy. The heart rate and other body processes of these animals become slow. Once these animals are out of hibernation they need to eat well. However, due to climate change, the food sources may not be available at that time. The scarcity of food during this crucial time often leads to starvation in these animals.

Brown Bears

Global warming is becoming a menace for brown bears as the winters are becoming warmer. As a result, bears are unable to go into hibernation. When they cannot hibernate, they become grouchy and aggressive. According to research in Spain, European brown bears living in the northern Cantabrian Mountains are not hibernating at all.

Confused Frogs

In Australia, the spotted snout-burrower frog hibernates in the dry Outback soil, awaiting the coming of rain. The reduction of consistent rain in the region, however, gives this amphibian mixed signals and has disrupted ancient patterns of hibernation and rebirth.

Marmots

Marmots are large ground squirrels found in the mountainous regions of Europe and Asia. They hibernate for eight months to avoid long winters and wake up when the climate becomes warm. This provides marmots a long growing season, which enhances their breeding and growth. Due to global warming, marmots are waking from hibernation almost 38 days earlier than usual.

Climate Facts

• Lemmings hibernate in burrows under the snow. They find it difficult to come out since unexpected rainfall has caused ice to deposit over their burrows.

• According to Italian scientists, dormice— small rodents known for their six-month long hibernation period—now hibernate five weeks less than they did two decades ago.

Climate Change Affects All

Global warming affects human beings as much as it affects other living organisms. Rising temperatures are responsible for drying up of lakes and rivers, leading to water shortage. Irregular rainfall is affecting agricultural production, leading to shortage of food.

Climatic Disturbances

Severe changes in climate have resulted in less rainfall and prolonged periods of droughts. It is also causing devastating wildfires. While some locations are experiencing dry and hot summers, others are facing frequent floods. In recent years, Britain has been hit by some of the worst floods it has ever seen. Some parts of the Northern Hemisphere now experience frequent heavy rains.

Threat to Humans

Deaths due to changes in temperatures, humidity, rainfall and snowfall patterns, and smog, are on the rise. High temperatures also favor the breeding of disease-carrying insects, such as mosquitoes. Mosquitoes causing **malaria** and **dengue fever** are now able to survive outside tropical regions and pose dangers to the health of people living in colder regions as well. According to the World Health Organization (WHO), one hundred fifty thousand people die every year due to problems related to climate change.

Invasive Species

Some living species are able to adapt to the changing climate. They leave their native place and move to new habitats to expand their range. These are called invasive species as they lead to the extinction of the native species by invading their habitats. Warm climate is causing the horse chestnut leaf miner (a leaf-mining moth) to migrate to the European countryside. Over the past ten years, chestnut trees have been attacked by these leaf miners, which feed on their leaves. As a result, the trees appear brown in color as each leaf is stained by the feeding scars left by these moths. The Colorado beetle has also spread to most of Europe and Russia, and has caused great destruction of potato crops.

Climate Facts

• Rising smog levels in the atmosphere could increase smog-related deaths by 80 percent in the next twenty years.

• In 2003, a summer heat wave in Europe killed thirty-five thousand people, especially in France where temperatures soared well above normal.

1. What is seagrass?

2. How do rising acid levels affect sealife?

3. What are amphibians?

4. Name some polar animals who are being affected by climate change.

5. How are bees impacted by the loss of flowers due to climate change?

6. What did a study say was happening to birds in Australia?

7. What habit of dormice is changing due to climate change?

8. What is one of the threats to human beings of biodiversity loss?

RESEARCH PROJECTS

1. Go online and find information about the world's largest coral reefs. Read articles about how climate change is affecting them. Then make a graph showing the change in size for each of the largest reefs over the past decades. Share your report with a group and brainstorm on some ways that we can help the decline in size of coral reefs.

2. Read more about how climate change and deforestation are affecting primates in Africa. Choose one species and research and present a report on how that animal's life is changing. What are humans doing to help this species? What do you think people should be doing?

3. Read about invasive species in your neighborhood or region. What species are moving in that should not be there? How are they affecting people in your area? What steps are being taken to combat this problem?

Books

Hansen, Thor. *Buzz: The Nature and Necessity of Bees.* New York: Basic Books, 2018.

McDonald, Joe. *Polar Bears In The Wild: A Visual Essay of an Endangered Species.* Amherst, MA: Amherst Media, 2018.

Sartore, Joel. *The Photo Ark: One Man's Quest to Document the World's Animals.* Washington D.C.: National Geographic, 2019.

On the Internet

Biodiversity Mapping
biodiversitymapping.org/wordpress/index.php/home/

National Geographic: Biodiversity
www.nationalgeographic.org/encyclopedia/
biodiversity/

UNESCO Biodiversity page
whc.unesco.org/en/biodiversity/

bioaccumulation the process of the buildup of toxic chemical substances in the body

biodiversity the diversity of plant and animal life in a habitat (or in the world as a whole)

ecosystem refers to a community of organisms, their interaction with each other, and their physical environment

famine a severe shortage of food (as through crop failure), resulting in hunger, starvation, and death

hydrophobic tending to repel and not absorb water or become wet by water

irrigation the method of providing water to agricultural fields

La Niña periodic, significant cooling of the surface waters of the equatorial Pacific Ocean, which causes abnormal weather patterns

migration the movement of persons or animals from one country or locality to another

pollutants the foreign materials which are harmful to the environment

precipitation the falling to earth of any form of water (rain, snow, hail, sleet, or mist)

stressors processes or events that cause stress

susceptible yielding readily to or capable of

symbiotic the interaction between organisms (especially of different species) that live together and happen to benefit from each other

vulnerable someone or something that can be easily harmed or attacked

INDEX

Photo Credits